SCHOLASTIC

writing guides

With interactive resources on CD-ROM

Poetry

for ages
7–9

Huw Thomas

Credits

Author
Huw Thomas

Development Editor
Marion Archer

Editor
Sarah Sodhi

Assistant Editor
Vicky Butt

Series Designer
Anna Oliwa

Designers
Paul Stockmans and
Liz Gilbert

Cover Illustration
Mark Oliver

Illustrations
Nigel Kitching and
Mike Phillips

CD-ROM Development
CD-ROM developed in
association with Infuze Ltd

Mixed Sources
Product group from well-managed
forests and other controlled sources
www.fsc.org Cert no. TT-COC-002769
© 1996 Forest Stewardship Council

Text © 2003, 2010 Huw Thomas
© 2010 Scholastic Ltd

Designed using Adobe InDesign

Published by Scholastic Ltd,
Book End
Range Road
Witney
Oxfordshire
OX29 0YD
www.scholastic.co.uk

Printed by Bell & Bain
1 2 3 4 5 6 7 8 9   0 1 2 3 4 5 6 7 8 9

British Library Cataloguing-in-Publication Data
A catalogue record for this book is available from the British Library.
ISBN 978-1407-11261-9

The rights of Huw Thomas to be identified as the author of this work has been asserted by him in accordance with the Copyright, Designs and Patents Act 1988.

Acknowledgments
The publishers gratefully acknowledge permission to reproduce the following copyright material: **Julius Kovac** for a quote from *Richard III*, Act 1: Scene 4 by William Shakespeare using the text from the website www.shakespeare.sk (from 2002 – untraceable); **The Peters Fraser and Dunlop Group Ltd** for the print use of the poem 'The Writer of this Poem' by Roger McGough from *Sky in the Pie* by Roger McGough © 1983 Roger McGough (1983 Kestrel); **United Agents** for the use of 'Babysitter' by Michael Rosen from *The Hypnotiser* by Michael Rosen © 1988, Michael Rosen (1988, Andre Deutsche); **United Agents** for the electronic use of the poem 'The Writer of this poem' by Roger McGough from *Sky in the Pie* by Roger McGough © 1983, Roger McGough (1983, Kestrel).
Every effort has been made to trace copyright holders for the works reproduced in this book, and the publishers apologise for any inadvertent omissions.

CD-ROM Minimum specifications:		
Windows 2000/XP/Vista	Mac OSX 10.4	
Processor: 1 GHz	RAM: 512 MB	Graphics card: 32bit
Audio card: Yes	CD-ROM drive speed: 8x	Hard disk space: 200MB
Screen resolution: 800x600		RM CC3

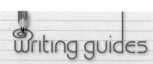

Contents

4 Introduction

5 How to use the CD-ROM

Section 1: Using good examples

7 Teachers' notes

Photocopiable extracts 1–3

10 Upon the Snail

11 The Writer of This Poem

12 Poem to Writer

Photocopiable activities

13 Which snail is which?

14 Simile mix-up

15 Poetry talk

16 To writers?

17 Which poem is which?

18 Working on a poem

Section 2: Developing writing

19 Teachers' notes

Photocopiable activities

25 Gathering words

26 Generating ideas

27 Concrete poems

28 Shape it

29 Line length

30 Metre

31 Fridge words

32 Alliteration challenge

33 Poem-scape

34 Image maker

Section 3: Writing

35 Teachers' notes

Photocopiable activities

38 Picking poetry

39 The poet's zig-zag

40 Stanza chunking

41 Stanza planner

42 Performing a poem

43 How do you say it?

Section 4: Review

44 Teachers' notes

Photocopiable activities

45 Self review

46 Peer review

47 Teacher review

Introduction: Poetry

The *Writing Guides* series aims to inspire and motivate children as writers by using creative approaches. Each *Writing Guide* contains activities and photocopiable resources designed to develop children's understanding of a particular genre (for example, fairy stories). The activities are in line with the requirements of the National Curriculum and the recommendations in the *Primary Framework for Literacy*. The teacher resource books are accompanied by a CD-ROM containing a range of interactive activities and resources.

What's in the book?

The *Writing Guides* series provides a structured approach to developing children's writing. Each book is divided into four sections.

Section 1: **Using good examples**
Three text extracts are provided to explore the typical features of the genre.

Section 2: **Developing writing**
There are ten short, focussed writing tasks in this section. These are designed to develop children's ability to use the key features of the genre in their own writing. The teachers' notes explain the objective of each activity and provide guidance on delivery, including how to use the photocopiable pages and the materials on the CD-ROM.

Section 3: **Writing**
The three writing projects in this section require the children to produce an extended piece of writing using the key features of the genre.

Section 4: **Review**
This section consists of a 'Self review', 'Peer review' and 'Teacher review'. These can be used to evaluate how effectively the children have met the writing criteria for the genre.

What's on the CD-ROM?

The accompanying CD-ROM contains a range of motivating activities and resources. The activities can be used for independent work or can be used on an interactive whiteboard to enhance group teaching.
Each CD-ROM contains:
- three text extracts that illustrate the typical features of the genre
- interactive versions of selected photocopiable pages
- four photographs and an audio file to create imaginative contexts for writing
- a selection of writing templates and images which can be used to produce extended pieces of writing.

The interactive activities on the CD-ROM promote active learning and support a range of teaching approaches and learning styles. For example, drag and drop and sequencing activities will support kinaesthetic learners.

Talk for writing

Each *Writing Guide* uses the principles of 'Talk for writing' to support children's writing development by providing opportunities for them to rehearse ideas orally in preparation for writing. 'Talk for writing' is promoted using a variety of teaching strategies including discussions, questioning and drama activities (such as, developing imaginative dialogue – see *Fantasy Stories for Ages 9–11*).

How to use the CD-ROM

Start screen: click on the 'Start' button to go to the main menu.

This section contains brief instructions on how to use the CD-ROM. For more detailed guidance, go to 'How to use the CD-ROM' on the start screen or click on the 'Help' button located in the top right-hand corner of the screen.

Installing the CD-ROM

Follow the instructions on the disk to install the CD-ROM onto your computer. Once the CD-ROM is installed, navigate to the program location and double click on the program icon to open it.

Main menu screen

Main menu

The main menu provides links to all of the writing activities and resources on the CD-ROM. Clicking on a button from the main menu will take you to a sub-menu that lists all of the activities and resources in that section. From here you have the option to 'Launch' the interactive activities, which may contain more than one screen, or print out the activities for pupils to complete by hand.

If you wish to return to a previous menu, click the 'Menu' button in the top right-hand corner of the screen; this acts as a 'back' button.

Screen tools

A range of simple writing tools that can be used in all of the writing activities are contained in the toolbar at the bottom of the screen.

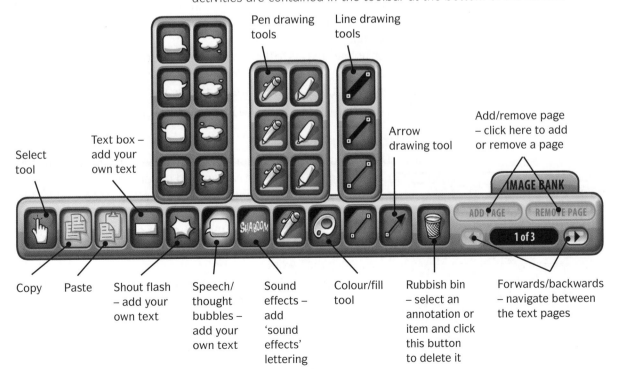

Pen drawing tools

Line drawing tools

Add/remove page – click here to add or remove a page

Arrow drawing tool

Select tool

Text box – add your own text

Copy

Paste

Shout flash – add your own text

Speech/ thought bubbles – add your own text

Sound effects – add 'sound effects' lettering

Colour/fill tool

Rubbish bin – select an annotation or item and click this button to delete it

Forwards/backwards – navigate between the text pages

How to use the CD-ROM

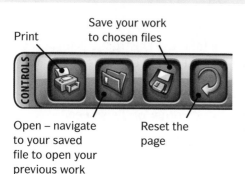

Print

Save your work to chosen files

Open – navigate to your saved file to open your previous work

Reset the page

Printing and saving work

All of the resources on the CD-ROM are printable. You can also save and retrieve any annotations made on the writing activities. Click on the 'Controls' tab on the right-hand side of the screen to access the 'Print', 'Open', 'Save' and 'Reset screen' buttons.

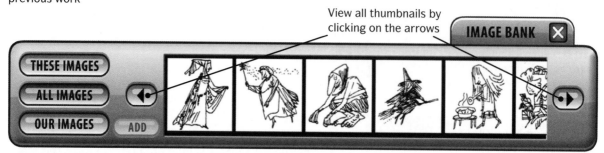

View all thumbnails by clicking on the arrows

Image bank – click and drag an image to add it to an activity

Image bank

Each CD-ROM has an 'Image bank' containing images appropriate to the genre being taught. Click on the tab at the bottom right of the screen to open the 'Image bank'. On the left-hand side there are three large buttons.

- The 'These images' button will display only the images associated with the specific activity currently open.
- The 'All images' button will display all the photographs and illustrations available on the CD-ROM.
- The 'Our images' button will contain any images you or the children have added to the CD-ROM.

Press the left or right arrows to scroll through the images available. Select an image and drag and drop it into the desired location on the screen. If necessary, resize the image using the arrow icon that appears at the bottom right of the image.

You can upload images to the 'Image bank', including digital photographs or images drawn and scanned into the computer. Click on 'Our images' and then 'Add' to navigate to where the image is stored. A thumbnail picture will be added to the gallery.

Writing your own story

Each CD-ROM contains a selection of blank writing templates. The fiction genre templates will be categorised under the button 'My story' and the non-fiction templates will be categorised under 'My recount' or 'My writing'. The writing templates encourage the children to produce an extended piece of genre writing. They can also add images, speech bubbles and use other tools to enhance their work.

The fiction titles also include a cover template for the children to use. They can customise their cover by adding their own title, blurb and images.

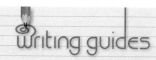

Section 1
Using good examples

Introduction to poetry

To write poetry you really do need to read it – read lots of it. Any teacher picking this up as a resource needs to gather some cracking good collections of poetry and read examples aloud to their class. The poems in this section are here as examples that prompt work throughout this guide. The poems span centuries and demonstrate the main elements of the genre.

Subject matter is vital when writing poetry – it needs to be something that inspires, strikes or riles. It is very hard to impose the subject of a poem on a class and you will do well to get them using the resources in Section 3 to find out what engages them. In Extract 1 a snail inspires John Bunyan. What will do the same for your young writers?

Word choices should take time. Poets take time finding the words that express their subject – whether it's the diverse adjectives of Extract 2 'The Writer of This Poem' or the beautiful verbs like 'goeth' and 'seizeth' with which Bunyan considers his snail.

The creative use of language is half the fun of poetry. Extract 2 'The Writer of This Poem' is an immodest list of similes, playing one big game with the reader, and Extract 3 'Poem to Writers' plays between instructions and poetry, about poetry. We need to emphasise this idea of poetry as creative fun with words. Imagery is a vital part of such word play – 'The Writer of This Poem' is made up of a whole host of images about the poet.

The crafting of lines is where we draw children towards some of the more technical aspects of the craft. We want them to think about how lines are shaped and said, appreciating their metrical structure. Tap out 'The Writer of This Poem' and the underlying rhythm presents a clear example of such sentence crafting at its lyrical best.

Links to the Primary Framework

The Literacy Framework provides detailed guidance for teaching and learning about poetry at Key Stage 2. In Years 3 and 4 poetry is explored in a variety of ways. This *Writing Guide* focuses on the following units from the Literacy Framework: Year 3 Poetry Unit 1 'Poems to perform'; Year 3 Poetry Unit 2 'Shape poetry and calligrams'; Year 4 Poetry Unit 1 'Creating images'; Year 4 Poetry Unit 2 'Exploring form'.

Poetry features

Subject
- Use of powerful or interesting subject matter.
- Selection of words for impact on reader.
- Descriptive words.

Creative use of language
- Word choices that make the reader look again.
- Use of imagery.

Crafting of lines
- Metrical structure of lines.
- Use of alliteration.

Section 1: Using good examples

Extract 1: Upon the Snail

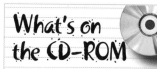

What's on the CD-ROM

Upon the Snail
- Text extract to read and discuss.

Which snail is which?
- Drag and drop snail statements to identify which occur in the poem.

Bunyan's poem takes a familiar animal, the common snail, and beautifies our appreciation of it.

- Before reading the poem, ask the children to think about words that describe the way snails move.

- Display 'Upon the Snail' from the CD-ROM or hand out photocopiable page 10. Ask the children to highlight details about the snail, stating which stanza they are referring to.

- Open 'Which snail is which?' from the CD-ROM and identify what Bunyan says about snails. Alternatively, use photocopiable page 13.

- Ask the children to pick out verbs from the poem and make a list on the board. In some cases they may have to guess that a word is an action, such as 'seizeth', 'procure' and 'gare' ('gare' means 'stare about'). Encourage the children to guess their meanings.

- Ask the children to pick out words that rhyme. They should see a clear pattern of first and third lines and second and fourth lines rhyming (ABAB). Can they also see rhymes shared by the third and first stanzas?

- Explain the use of alliteration in poems – that is, the repeated use of a consonant sound to add to the musical quality of the lines. Pick out the use of the 's' sound (sometimes blended to a 'sh').

Extract 2: The Writer of This Poem

What's on the CD-ROM

The Writer of This Poem
- Text extract to read and discuss.

Poetry talk
- Identify which poem the comments refer to.
- Roll over the comments to reveal question prompts.

Roger McGough's poem takes the form of a list.

- Display 'The Writer of This Poem' from the CD-ROM or hand out photocopiable page 11. Explain that some poems present a list of thoughts or ideas around a subject. Ask the children to consider what the subject is and to find things the poem says about this subject.

- Explain the way a simile is structured – a subject is likened to another thing using the structure: 'As [adjective] as [noun]'.

- Looking through this poem, ask the children to pick out a simile and explain how the adjective links with the noun. For example, a nib (noun) is clearly sharp (adjective), but in what ways is the north wind keen?

- Read the poem again, asking the children to try to remember as many of the similes as they can. Then re-read the poem to the children while they cannot see the words. Can they finish off some of the lines?

- Using photocopiable page 14 'Simile mix-up', ask the class to match up these broken similes and place them in the correct order.

- Then open 'Poetry talk' from the CD-ROM and pick out questions to prompt a class discussion about Extracts 1 and 2. Photocopiable page 15 offers a simpler version of this activity, without question prompts.

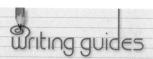

Extract 3: Poem to Writers

What's on the CD-ROM

Poem to Writers
- Text extract to read, discuss and edit.

Poetry rules
- Drag the arrows to identify the poet's opinion on each rule.

This poem expresses one poet's thoughts on the rules of writing poetry.

- Begin by asking the children if they have any thoughts about the writing of poems. Ask: *Are there any guides or normal rules in poetry?* List a few of these orally and hold them in mind as you display and read Extract 3 'Poem to Writers' from the CD-ROM or photocopiable page 12.

- Ask the children to work in pairs, looking at the poem and picking out what they think this writer is putting forward as guidance for poetry. As they pick these out, annotate the on-screen version. Revisit their own list of advice – are any of their thoughts evident in the poem?

- Open 'Poetry rules' on the CD-ROM and read through the list. Encourage the children to express their views on what they feel about each of these guidelines.

- Drag the arrows to sort the statements into those they think are supported by the poem and those that are not. Some are trickier than others, for example the rule 'Write quickly' could be supported by the line 'don't hold back' but there is also conflict with this rule where the poet says 'Comfort calls'.

- Once they have done this as a shared task, invite the children to work on photocopiable page 16 'Poetry rules' in pairs.

Poster: Working on a poem

What's on the CD-ROM

Working on a poem
- Roll over the points about poetry to reveal links to the three poems.

The poster draws together the ideas about poetry examined in this section. It also prompts the children to think about editing their work.

- Display the poster 'Working on a poem' from the CD-ROM and hand out photocopiable page 18. Read through the poster with copies of the three poems – divide the class into three groups and give each group one poem to explore. (It helps if they have already tried the 'Poetry talk' activity on photocopiable page 15.)

- Ask the children if they can identify features in their group's poem that are mentioned on the poster.

- Then roll over the bubbles to reveal examples from the poems relating to the different points. When examining points in the second bubble explain that the poems do not all rhyme – nor do they have to.

- Invite the children to use their memory to sort the elements on photocopiable page 17 'Which poem is which?' according to the poem they are from.

- Encourage the children to refer to this poster (photocopiable page 18) as they work through the activities in Section 2, which build on these ideas, and as they compose their own poems in Section 3.

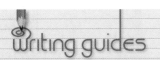
writing guides

Extract 1: Upon the Snail

She goes softly, but she goeth sure;
She stumbles not as stronger creatures do:
Her journey's shorter, so she may endure
Better than they which do much further go.

She makes no noise, but stilly seizeth on
The flower or herb appointed for her food,
The which she quietly doth feed upon,
While others range, and gare, but find no good.

And though she doth but very softly go,
However 'tis not fast, nor slow, but sure;
And certainly they that do travel so,
The prize they do aim at, they do procure.

John Bunyan

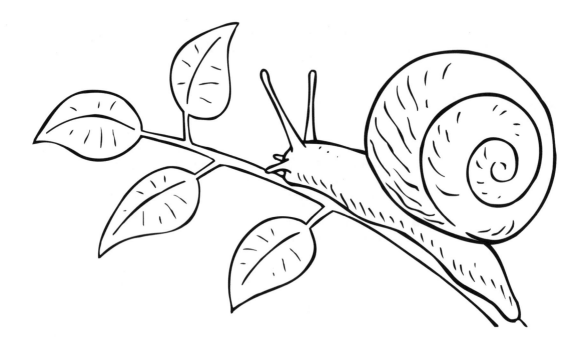

Writing guides

Extract 2: The Writer of This Poem

The writer of this poem
Is taller than a tree
As keen as the North Wind
As handsome as can be

As bold as a boxing-glove
As sharp as a nib
As strong as scaffolding
As tricky as a fib

As smooth as a lolly-ice
As quick as a lick
As clean as a chemist-shop
As clever as a ✔

The writer of this poem
Never ceases to amaze
He's one in a million billion
(or so the poem says!)

Roger McGough

Text © 1983, Roger McGough; illustration © 2003, Nigel Kitching.

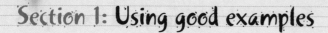

Extract 3: Poem to Writers

Hey
You with the pen.
Sharpen your lines
Shape it like you say it.

And
don't hold back
With the words
Which you're wanting.

Comfort
calls and calling crackles
in this happy craft.

You are a poet.
Everyone else can take a running
Jump.

Illustration © 2010, Mike Phillips/Beehive Illustration.

writing guides

SCHOLASTIC www.scholastic.co.uk **Photocopiable**

Which snail is which?

- Which of these statements about snails does the poem tell us?
- Which of them are not from the poem?
- Cut them out and sort the statements into two piles.

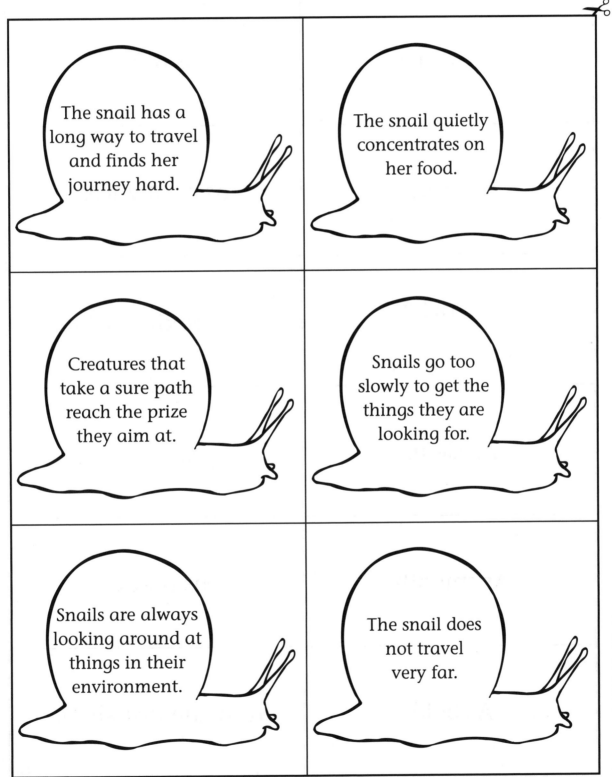

The snail has a long way to travel and finds her journey hard.

The snail quietly concentrates on her food.

Creatures that take a sure path reach the prize they aim at.

Snails go too slowly to get the things they are looking for.

Snails are always looking around at things in their environment.

The snail does not travel very far.

Illustrations © 2003, Nigel Kitching.

Simile mix-up

● Match these mixed-up similes and rearrange them as they appear in 'The Writer of This Poem'.

As sharp	as a fib.
As quick	as a lolly-ice.
As tricky	as a boxing-glove.
As clean	as a nib.
As smooth	as a lick.
As bold	as a chemist-shop.

writing guides

Poetry talk

● Here are some comments from children about 'Upon the Snail' and 'The Writer of This Poem'. Under each comment write down the poem it refers to.

It was full of
good similes.

_____

It made you look
again at something you see
so much.

_____

It sounded a bit
old fashioned.

_____

The language was
hard to understand.

_____

I thought it was
a funny poem.

_____

I thought it was
a strange subject
for a poem.

_____

The last verse was
big headed.

_____

The lines felt long
and musical.

_____

Illustration © 2003, Nigel Kitching.

Section 1: Using good examples

Poetry rules

- Read 'Poem to Writers' then look at the rules about writing poetry. Which ones do you think the poet would agree with and which are nonsense? Cut them out and arrange them into two piles.

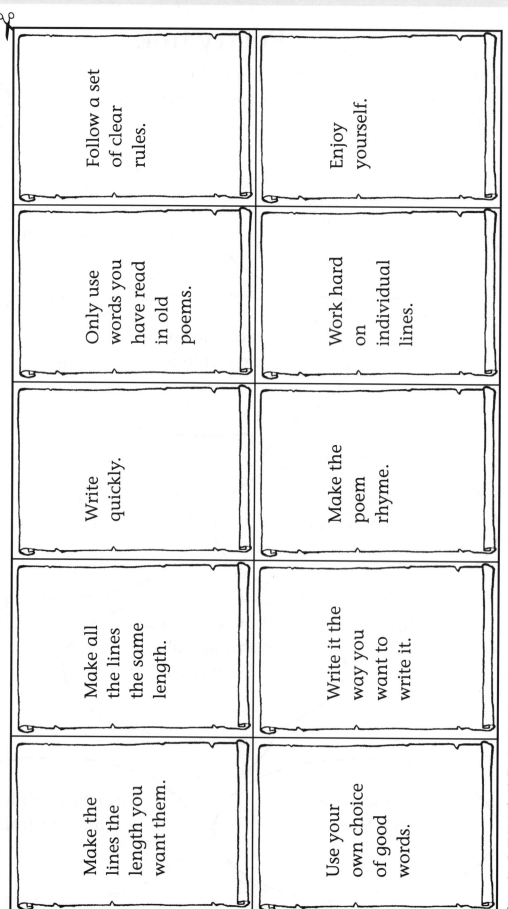

Follow a set of clear rules.

Only use words you have read in old poems.

Write quickly.

Make all the lines the same length.

Make the lines the length you want them.

Enjoy yourself.

Work hard on individual lines.

Make the poem rhyme.

Write it the way you want to write it.

Use your own choice of good words.

Illustration © 2010, Mike Phillips/Beehive Illustration.

writing guides

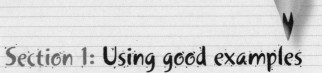

Which poem is which?

● Without looking at the poems, cut out and sort these 'images in words', 'interesting words' and 'thoughts about the subject' into three piles, one for each of the three poems.

Images in words	animals going fast and missing some food	*images*
	being keener than the North Wind	*images*
	poetry writing being a craft	*images*
	sharpening a line of writing like a tool	*images*
	the snail going on a short but sure journey	*images*
	the strength of scaffolding	*images*
Interesting words	as tricky as a fib	*words*
	calling crackles	*words*
	others range, and gare	*words*
	sharpen your lines	*words*
	so the poem says	*words*
	the prize they do aim at, they do procure	*words*
Thoughts about the subject	a poem saying its own writer is amazing	*subject*
	poets can write what they want to write	*subject*
	it's better to be a slow steady food finder than go quick and hungry	*subject*
	a simile in nearly every line	*subject*
	snails go slow so find more food	*subject*
	you need to work hard choosing the words you use in poetry writing	*subject*

Section 1: Using good examples

Working on a poem

● Collect or find...

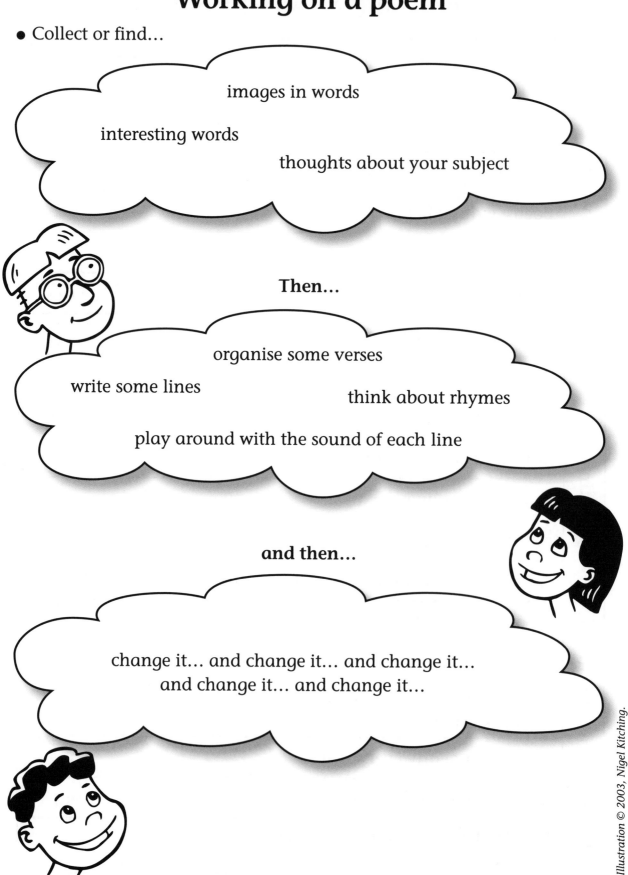

images in words

interesting words

thoughts about your subject

Then...

organise some verses

write some lines

think about rhymes

play around with the sound of each line

and then...

change it... and change it... and change it... and change it... and change it...

Illustration © 2003, Nigel Kitching.

Section 2
Developing writing

Activities breakdown

Word choice
- Gathering words (page 20)
- Generating ideas (page 20)
- Fridge words (page 23)
- Alliteration challenge (page 23)

Subject matter
- Gathering words (page 20)
- Generating ideas (page 20)
- Poem-scape (page 24)
- Image maker (page 24)

Creative use of language
- Shape it (page 21)
- Beat shapes (page 21)
- Line length (page 22)
- Fridge words (page 23)

Crafting of lines
- Shape it (page 21)
- Beat shapes (page 21)
- Line length (page 22)
- Metre (page 22)
- Alliteration challenge (page 23)

Imagery
- Shape it (page 21)
- Fridge words (page 23)
- Poem-scape (page 24)
- Image maker (page 24)

In this section, skills of composition and language use are honed, leading into the actual writing of poetry. There is an initial exploration of how to gather words around a subject, with the aim of finding the best words for use in a poem. Photocopiable page 33 'Poem-scape' performs a similar task, and the questions in the interactive version on the CD-ROM will enhance this.

Subject matter
It is important that children have a subject matter to write about. There are no activities specifically to deliver this – you need to promote subjects from the children's own experiences and the ideas they bring. Throughout this section, however, ideas are suggested for using the images in the 'Media resources' section of the CD-ROM, which can be used to stimulate ideas across all the activities. For example, activities on metre need a starting point, so why not use the 'Fire' image to spark this off?

Creative use of language
Having gathered words, children then need the freedom poetry allows to use these in creative ways. The 'Fridge words' activity (on page 23) serves both as an activity in itself but also models a way of working with words, shuffling them around to create interesting wording. Emphasise throughout the activities that children can play with the language and have fun with it.

Crafting of lines
Work on syllables and metre can get very complex. The activities here present a simple way of exploring this area using beats in lines. We shape them, beat them out and use metre. There is also an emphasis on how things are to be said, which will be developed further in Section 3 when we look at performance of poetry. This section also explores alliteration, emphasising the importance of listening to how a line sounds.

Imagery
Part of the construction of poetry involves the devising of imagery. Keep children focused on the purpose of this device as imagery has a significant impact. The activities here use compact and focused texts that are well crafted and redrafted to make for lively and interesting words.

Activity 1: Gathering words

Objective

To choose and combine words, images and other features for particular effects. (Year 4 Strand 9)

What's on the CD-ROM

Media resources
- Display the 'Fire', 'Snail' and 'Cityscape' images to inspire ideas.

What to do
This activity focuses on gathering language, the starting place for developing children's writing.

- Ask the children to work in groups of three. Provide each child with photocopiable page 25 'Gathering words' and ask each group to choose an object to write about. Provide objects, such as shells or leaves, and the images from the CD-ROM as inspiration.

- Working individually, ask the children to fill the word spaces in the centre of the photocopiable sheet with words and phrases that their object or picture evokes. These could describe what they see, or comment on their experience of it. Stress that half the fun lies in not seeing each other's ideas at this stage.

- Let the children consult with the rest of their group to compile a list of six words or phrases drawn from all three lists. They should select the words and phrases they think are doing a powerful or poetic job.

- Prompt the children individually to use these words to compile a short piece of free verse about their object or picture. This could simply be the list of words they have compiled – sometimes these alone will make evocative descriptions.

Activity 2: Generating ideas

Objective

To show imagination through the language used to create emphasis, humour, atmosphere or suspense.
(Year 4 Strand 9)

What's on the CD-ROM

Generating ideas
- Type ideas about sensory memories of an experience.

Media resources
- Display the 'Cityscape' image to inspire ideas.

What to do
This activity highlights the senses, which are a vibrant way to communicate experience.

- Open 'Generating ideas' from the CD-ROM. Ask the children to recall a recent, shared experience. If needed, suggest some examples, such as a visit to a swimming pool, a bus trip or a really hot day.

- Ask the children to close their eyes and conjure up the memory in their minds. Tell them to think through the images they would see, the noises they would hear and the smells they would encounter. They will need time and silence to go through this. Ask the children to share their thoughts and use the spaces on the screen to record examples.

- Invite the children to imagine they are walking through the situation. Ask: *What would you touch? What would it feel like?* Again, share ideas and make notes on screen.

- Finally, are there any tastes the children can associate with this memory or other words they could use to describe the experience?

- Ask the children to individually complete photocopiable page 26 'Generating ideas'. They can either use the same stimulus, one of their own or the 'Cityscape' image on the CD-ROM (remember, there are things to taste in a city!).

Activity 3: Shape it

Objective

To choose and combine words, images and other features for particular effects. (Year 4 Strand 9)

What's on the CD-ROM

Media resources
- Display the 'Punishment' image to inspire concrete poetry.

What to do

This activity is about concrete poetry, evoking and playing with language to stimulate writing.

- Explain that a concrete poem is a poem in which the layout of the words represents an aspect of the subject.

- On the board, write the sentences from photocopiable page 27 'Concrete poems' as you normally would. Ask the children to work in groups, thinking how they could turn these into concrete poems.

- Share thoughts about this. Point out that a concrete poem is not just words in the shape of their subject – the best ones make the reading move in a way that matches the subject.

- Show the children photocopiable page 27 and see whether the children's versions are similar to these.

- Think of concrete lines for the children to try, such as 'I fell over' and 'The balloon burst'. Also, show them the 'Punishment' image of the child being told off in the 'Media resources' section of the CD-ROM. How could they write a line in concrete form to show words are shouted?

- Stress that the idea is not simply to jam words into a shape; they need to think of the movement of a subject or the features of it.

- Give the children photocopiable page 28 'Shape it' to create their own concrete poems.

Activity 4: Beat shapes

Objective

To choose and combine words, images and other features for particular effects. (Year 4 Strand 9)

What to do

This activity begins the work on metre in poetry.

- Revise the concept of syllables with the children. Ask them to clap out the number of beats in a word.

- Ask the children to choose a subject to put into writing. Then invite them to write about their subject using a specific beat structure, such as 2/2/7/7/2/2. They should aim to make these short and self-contained lines. For example: 'Sun rise / Red glow'. They then need two longer lines, allowing more extended language, such as: 'Walking into the morning'.

- Point out that the full effect is not just in the look of the words on the page; the line length also affects the way in which we 'read' the poem. Emphasise to the children that, as they do this task, they are shaping the sound as well as the look of the poem.

- Encourage them to try other beat structures, either with different subjects or the same subject in different shapes. They could also try to work out the syllable number and line length for varying shapes.

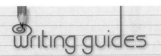

Activity 5: Line length

Objective

To make decisions about form and purpose, identify success criteria and use them to evaluate their writing. (Year 3 Strand 9)

What's on the CD-ROM

Line length
- Type in revised line lengths.

What to do

This activity looks at how the length of a line influences how we read and say it.

- Open 'Line length' from the CD-ROM and read the first line together. Ask: *Where would you cut this line to turn it into two lines?* Demonstrate different possibilites by typing in the revised lines.

- Give the children photocopiable page 29 'Line length' to experiment with different options. Ask volunteers to read their own version aloud to the class. Having tried one divided over two lines, invite them to make a second version over three lines.

- Point out the way in which reading aloud brings the impression of the lines home to the reader. Let the children continue making third and fourth cuts, arranging the lines in different ways.

- Once the children have the example they want, tell them to stick it down on a separate piece of paper. They can then try this approach with some of the other lines of text on the photocopiable sheet.

Activity 6: Metre

Objective

To develop and refine ideas in writing using planning and problem-solving strategies. (Year 4 Strand 9)

What's on the CD-ROM

Upon the Snail
- Text extract to read and discuss.

Metre
- Drag and drop metric beats next to the correct lines of poetry.

What to do

This activity explores how metre gives poetry a distinctive rhythm, created by the number of syllables in each line.

- Show the children Extract 1 'Upon the Snail' from the CD-ROM. Count the first ten syllables in the lines. When reading aloud, the reader soon falls in with the rhythm of these lines.

- Ask the children to tap out a rhythm as you read – sounding positively like a dee-dum, dee-dum, dee-dum, dee-dum, dee-dum.

- Mark this by annotating the lines of the poem on the board, as shown below:

X	/	X	/	X	/	X	/	X	/
She	go	eth	soft	ly	but	she	go	eth	sure

X	/	X	/	X	/	X	/	X	/
She	stum	bles	not	as	stron	ger	creat	ures	do

- Each dee-dum is known as a metrical foot. Bunyan's poem has lines of five feet. This structure is called a pentameter.

- Ask the children to cut out and read the lines shown on photocopiable page 30 'Metre' and sort them into those with two beats, four beats and so on, grouping them together with those of the same number of beats. Point out that lines in a poem can have a varied metre.

- Open 'Metre' on the CD-ROM and ask the children to pool their findings as you undertake this as a whole-class activity.

Activity 7: Fridge words

Objective

To choose and combine words, images and other features for particular effects. (Year 4 Strand 9)

What's on the CD-ROM

Fridge words
- Click on words to highlight them.
- Rearrange and type in the selected words to create a poetic line.

What to do

This activity draws on the popular concept of fridge magnet poetry, in which language is shuffled to produce interesting effects.

- Open 'Fridge words' from the CD-ROM and silently play with the words, clicking on and typing in different combinations. Let the children read what you create. Start with a noun and gather words around it. Be adventurous and do not worry too much about sense – 'flickering sky' sounds good!

- Distribute copies of photocopiable page 31 'Fridge words' and ask the children to cut out the words. Suggest to the children that, starting with one of the central nouns (for example 'friend') and an opening word (for example 'my'), they can use the other words to create brilliant lines (for example 'My gentle friend is thundering').

- Encourage them to change words in lines they have made, such as changing 'friend' for 'sky', and seeing how that sounds.

- They should note down any striking lines they create. Stress that they do not need their lines to make perfect sense to be considered worth recording (for example 'My slender night is whispering').

Activity 8: Alliteration challenge

Objective

To choose and combine words, images and other features for particular effects. (Year 4 Strand 9)

What's on the CD-ROM

Upon the Snail
- Text extract to read and discuss.

What to do

This activity explores alliteration as a great way to stimulate children's experiments in combining the sound and meaning of words.

- Ask the children to select a letter of the alphabet and then think of a subject that begins with the letter, such as 'd' and 'dog'. Can they think of an adjective beginning with the same letter that describes the subject ('dirty dog')? Explain that this is alliteration – the repeated use of the same consonant sound in a number of words in close proximity.

- Read the first lines of Extract 1 'Upon the Snail' from the CD-ROM. Point out the 's' or 'sh' sounds, which create an alliteration effect.

- Hand out photocopiable page 32 'Alliteration challenge'. Working in pairs, ask the children to rebuild the alliterative lines. Invite them to sort similar initial sounds, then rebuild them into meaningful lines.

- Challenge the children to write a line in which more than half the words contain the same sound as the first word (for example 'dirty dog didn't distress us today'). Let them try again with a second line, creating an alliterative couplet.

- Ask the children to write the lines of text in different-coloured pens, using the same colour for the alliterative sound.

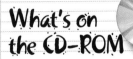

Activity 9: Poem-scape

Objective

To clarify meaning and point of view by using varied sentence structure (phrases, clauses and adverbials).
(Year 4 Strand 11)

What's on the CD-ROM

Media resources
- Display the four images to stimulate discussion.

Poem-scape
- Roll over the text to reveal question prompts to help create a poem.

What to do

This activity focuses on poetry evoked by a particular stimulus.

- Invite the children to think of a subject or theme, or use the four images from the 'Media resources' section of the CD-ROM as stimuli.

- Hand out photocopiable page 33 'Poem-scape' for the children to complete individually. Ask them to note their subject in the centre.

- Open 'Poem-scape' from the CD-ROM and as they are working, stop them occasionally and refer to the roll-over text to stimulate further thinking.

- After gathering notes, ask them to write an opening stanza that sets the scene, taking thoughts and words from each of the four sections to build up an impression of their chosen subject, for example:

> Lost in town,
> thinking where's Mum?
> Scared.
> Bustling crowds
> as I look in the shop windows.

- Let the children return to the subject and use the same structure to produce more lines or verses for their poem.

Activity 10: Image maker

Objective

To clarify meaning and point of view by using varied sentence structure (phrases, clauses and adverbials).
(Year 4 Strand 11)

What's on the CD-ROM

Media resources
- Display the four images to stimulate discussion.

What to do

This activity explores the imagery inherent in poetry.

- Distribute photocopiable page 34 'Image maker'. Ask the children to think of a subject (for example, an object, a feeling or an experience) or use the four images on the CD-ROM to stimulate ideas.

- Explain how to use the image maker. They should write their subject in a space on the first row. Underneath they will write a quality of the subject, for example: 'Being lost – confusing'.

- Explain that they will need to think of something else that shares the same quality and write that in the third row, for example: 'Being lost – confusing – a crossword puzzle'.

- Finally, consider other thoughts about the things recorded in rows one and three. For example, a further similarity ('clues can provide answers') or a further image ('streets look like crossword lines').

- Having done this, they will have generated an image that could be used in various ways, for example:

> Lost like a confused puzzler
> I was lost. It was like a baffling crossword.
> Lost in a crossword town.

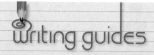

Gathering words

• Write your chosen object in the handle. Then record words and phrases linked to your object inside the shopping basket.

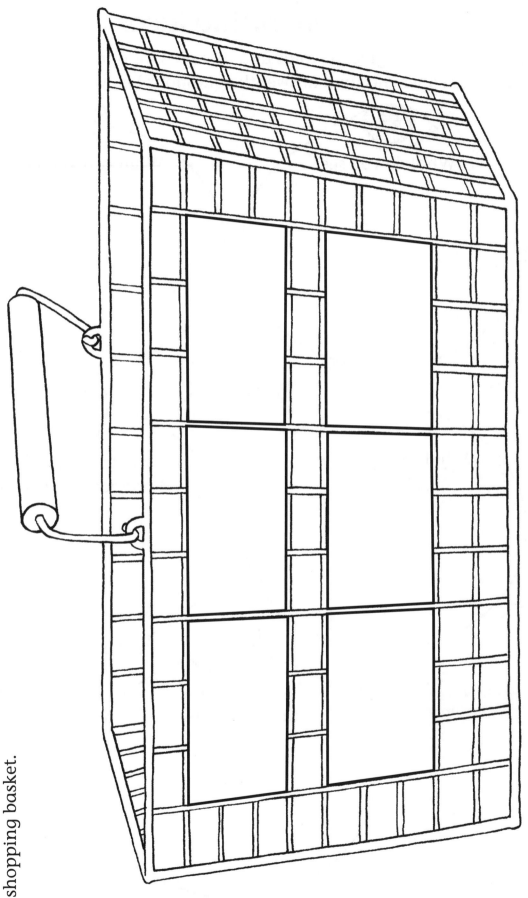

Illustration © 2010, Mike Phillips/Beehive Illustration.

Section 2: Developing writing

Generating ideas

● Our senses can give us words and thoughts for our poems. Think about an experience and answer the questions below.

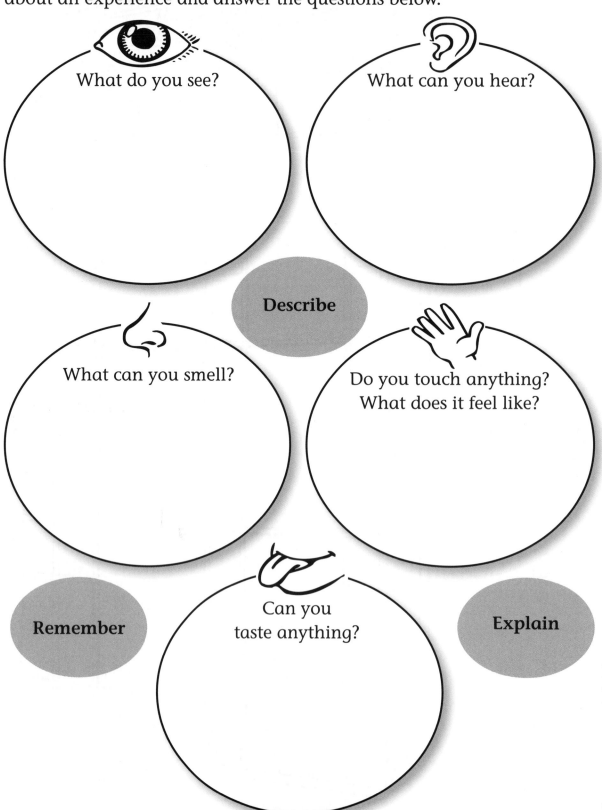

What do you see?

What can you hear?

Describe

What can you smell?

Do you touch anything? What does it feel like?

Remember

Can you taste anything?

Explain

Illustration © 2003, Nigel Kitching.

Concrete poems

● How do these short, concrete poems use their shape to match their subject? Would you shape them differently? Suggest possible changes to the shape of these poems.

Tackle

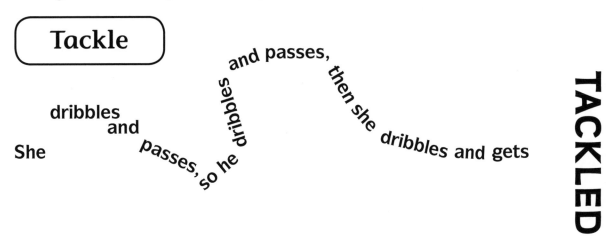

Splashing

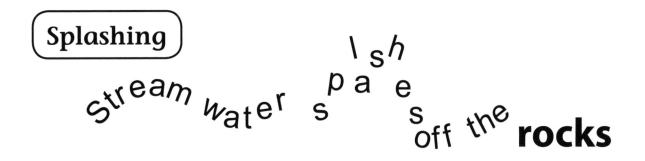

Lost and found

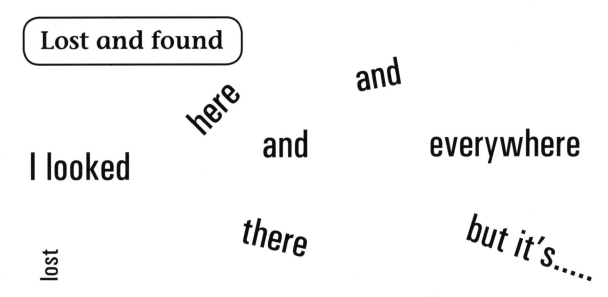

Shape it

● Turn these short lines into concrete poems.

Raindrops are falling from the sky

Your angry shouting

Cars are speedy

Line length

● Cut out a line of text and snip it to create one, two, three or more lines.
● Try different line lengths with the other lines of text.

Drops of rain are snaking down my window.
Cars painfully plod through the city streets.
My brother chased me, screaming, up the stairs.
Suddenly I heard a tapping on the window.
In the hot rain I stopped to watch a snail slither along my path.
Because I wasn't looking I tripped down the steps and stubbed my toe.

Metre

- Cut out and sort the lines into different metric beats.

'Twas brillig, and the slithy toves

Did gyre and gimble in the wabe:

Lewis Carroll

Lord! Lord! Methought what pain it was to drown!

What dreadful noise of waters in mine ears!

William Shakespeare

Whenever the moon and stars are set,

Whenever the wind is high,

Robert Louis Stevenson

Does the road wind up-hill all the way?

Yes, to the very end.

Christina Rossetti

They went to sea in a Sieve, they did,

In a Sieve they went to sea:

Edward Lear

Listen…

With faint dry sound,

Like steps of passing ghosts,

Adelaide Crapsey

'Tis moonlight, summer moonlight,

All soft and still and fair;

The solemn hour of midnight

Breathes sweet thoughts everywhere,

Emily Brontë

William Shakespeare's text is from the website www.shakespeare.sk (from 2002 – untraceable).

Fridge words

● Cut out each word. Select at least one word from each pattern category and use them to create a poetic line.

the	a	my	this
beautiful	gentle	slender	open
cold	lonely	fresh	bright
night	cat	sky	sea
sun	air	friend	candle
is	was	appears	comes
falling	rising	flickering	thundering
creeping	glowing	sleeping	whispering

Illustration © 2003, Nigel Kitching.

Photocopiable  SCHOLASTIC
www.scholastic.co.uk

Alliteration challenge

● Looking out for the alliteration, put these jumbled lines back together.

Beginning	Middle	End
Pass the	falls from	wave that wand!
The dirty dog	crashes the	in the late sun.
The crazy clown	plate of	a fruit tree.
Freaky fox	loll around	delightfully.
Watch the	dances	pickles and prunes.
Lazy lions	window when you	colourful car.

writing guides

Poem-scape

● Write a subject in the middle and use the prompts around to help you think of lines for your poem.

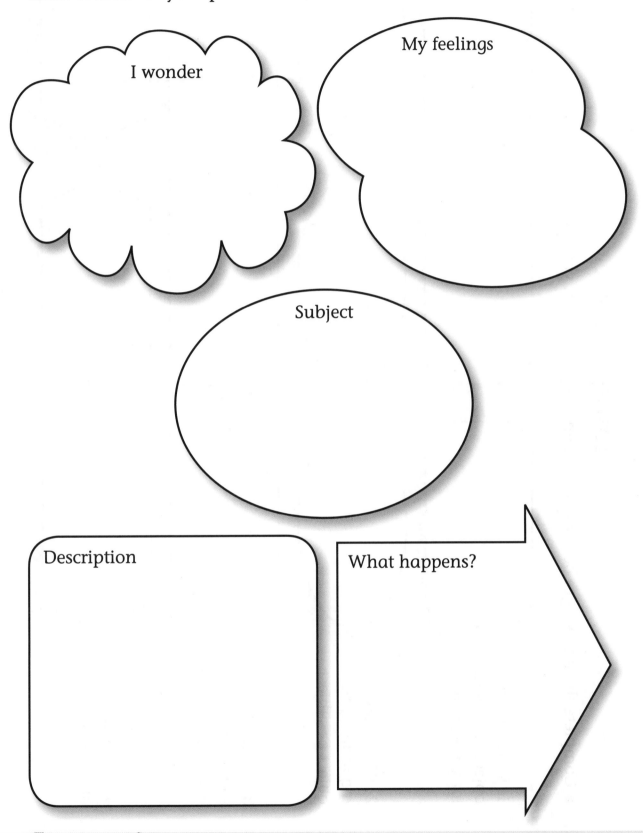

I wonder

My feelings

Subject

Description

What happens?

Image maker

● Complete the four stages below to create an image to use in your poem.

1. Start with an object or subject for your poem.

2. Write down a quality of the object or subject.

3. Think of something else with that quality.

4. Write down other thoughts.

Writing

In this section the children are encouraged to draw from material that they have worked on in Section 2 and use it in their own composition.

The projects take children through the three stages of the writing process, but maintain a focus on writing. Poetry is one of the most intensely concentrated types of writing in which young writers will engage. It involves gathering more material than they will use and a conscious structuring, not just of the words used, but also the length of lines, the sounds they make and the way the lines connect. The initial project develops this idea of gathering a lot of material. In this, as in all poetry writing, the message is 'less is more'. Children can gather a great deal of material but concentrating it down to a punchy, succinct piece of writing will bring their poems to life. To assist with the information gathering, direct the children to the various places from which they may gather stimuli. Ideally, encourage them to use experiences they have outside school – from home or from a school outing that stimulates their imagination. The fieldwork is essential.

Having gathered a range of material, the children then need the poetic discipline of organising it. Project 2 'Stanza chunking' provides a means of shaping their ideas in a way that matches their thoughts to one of the most basic structures of poetry – the stanza. Again, the emphasis should be on short and focused development of stanzas that take a subject and deal with it in different ways.

So much of what was covered in Section 2, to do with metre and line length, is really experienced when a reader fully engages with the lyricism and sounds of lines of poetry. Project 3 'Writing for performance' picks up on this essential aspect of poetry by promoting the notion of performance. Any poem can be recited or performed, but the emphasis here is on constructing a poem where the language lends itself to performance. This can be through the way things are said and also through devising opportunities for audience participation. Keep the focus on material that will work in this context and make sure material constructed for performance actually gets performed.

Using the writing templates

The 'My poem' writing templates allow the children to produce their own poetry using images and text. They can type their poems directly into one of the writing templates or the writing templates can be printed out for the children to fill in by hand. There is a selection of images available in the 'Image bank' that can be incorporated into the writing templates to illustrate their poems. It is also possible for the children to upload their own images into the 'Our images' section of the 'Image bank' (see the 'Help file' on the CD-ROM for more details).

Writing tips

- Gather more material than you need.
- Listen to how your lines will sound.
- Gather the best words from a wide range of possibilities.
- Construct interesting lines of poetry.
- Organise your material.
- Think how your poem will sound when read aloud.

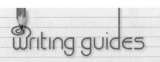

Project 1: Picking poetry

What to do

This project develops ideas from the gathering stage onwards.

- Distribute photocopiable page 38 'Picking poetry'. Explain that they need to use the card to gather ideas and language to use in their poetry. Ideally they should use this card over a few days, either in school or outside. It works well over a weekend.

- Photocopiable page 39 'The poet's zig-zag' provides a toolkit for creating a poem. Use 'The poet's zig-zag' from the CD-ROM both to show how it works and also what John Bunyan's zig-zag may have looked for 'Upon the Snail'.

- Ask the children to read ideas from their 'Picking poetry' note card and use these ideas to complete their own zig-zag.

- The second section of the zig-zag provides a space to write some vocabulary, so invite them to generate a list that they can draw from. The third section is devoted to imagery and the use of the senses, where the children may use the similes and metaphors devised in Section 2. In the final section, the children need to construct a verse of their poem, beginning the process of creating lengthier works.

- Finally, the children need to use their notes to write a poem on the subject they have chosen using the 'My poem' writing templates.

Project 2: Stanza chunking

What to do

As they develop in their planning and writing of poems, children need to take the skills they have worked on in Section 2 and begin to write more extended verses. This project uses stanzas as a way of gathering ideas into separate and extended chunks of a poem.

- Explain that the first steps to writing poetry are: jotting down thoughts about a subject and organising them. Then open 'Stanza chunking' from the CD-ROM and click on each thought bubble to reveal questions designed to stimulate thoughts to explore in a poem.

- Distribute photocopiable page 40 'Stanza chunking'. Ask the children to try their own stanza chunking ideas, gathering their thoughts into a plan for a three- or four-stanza poem.

- Working in fours, ask the children to bring their notes together. Hand out photocopiable page 41 'Stanza planner' and let them discuss the questions and make further notes. Encourage them to review their own poetry planning in light of each question.

- Invite the children to use the ideas they have gathered to write a poem, formed into stanzas, using the 'My poem' writing templates. Prompt the children to ask themselves: *What am I doing in each stanza?*

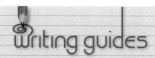

Project 3: Writing for performance

Objectives

To identify features that writers use to provoke readers' reactions.
(Year 3 Strand 8)
To show imagination through the language used to create emphasis, humour, atmosphere or suspense.
(Year 4 Strand 9)

What's on the CD-ROM

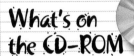

Media resources
● Listen to the audio clip of a poet performing a poem.

Performing a poem
● Type in notes to plan a poem for performance.

My poem
● Compose a performance poem using the writing templates.

What to do

This project emphasises the performance and recitation of poetry, linking preparation to presentation.

● Play the children the audio clip of a poet performing a poem, listening to how she says the lines.

● Explain that they are going to write a poem that would be good to perform.

● Open 'Performing a poem' from the CD-ROM and together use this as a means of modelling a class performance idea. They could write a poem about what teachers say as they arrive every morning, possibly even trying some voices.

● When the children understand the process hand out photocopiable page 42 'Performing a poem' to use as the main stimulus in starting their own poem for performance.

● Turn their attention to the section on the right-hand side, which gives an opportunity to make notes about how a performance of this poem could work. Work out who says what and decide which actions go with certain lines. The main aim here is for the children to have a planned understanding of how their performance will work.

● Using photocopiable page 43 'How do you say it?', ask the children to think of four points in their performance poem that they will say in a particular way. It could be a voice they adopt for that line or using a particular rhythm. Can they describe how it will be said? The activities 'Beat shapes' (page 21) and 'Line length' (page 22) may help.

● Using their notes, ask the children to write a poem using the 'My poem' writing templates.

● Finally, provide each child with the opportunity to perform their poem in front of the class.

Photocopiable SCHOLASTIC www.scholastic.co.uk

Picking poetry

- Fold the poetry picker into a card.
- Use this note card to gather ideas for a poem.

Things people say	Things I could write about
How I feel	What things look like

The poet's zig-zag

• Fill in the four sections to gather some thoughts for a poem.

Images: what your subject makes you think of

Some lines about your subject

Tap out that metre!

Words that you can use about your subject (for example, adjectives to describe, interesting verbs, different names for something)

Sense words: smells, sights or sounds

The **poet's** zig-zag

for a poem about

What started you working on this idea?

Photocopiable **SCHOLASTIC** www.scholastic.co.uk

Stanza chunking

● Gather and organise ideas to form stanzas in a poem.

The subject of your poem is _____

Thoughts about your subject.

● Now plan three or four stanzas about your subject.

1. _____   3. _____

_____   _____

_____   _____

2. _____   4. _____

_____   _____

_____   _____

Writing guides

Stanza planner

● Think about these questions. Make notes as you plan and compose your stanzas.

Could some stanzas give more detail? Look closer at an aspect?	Did something move or change during the poem?
Is there something special to keep until the final stanza?	Can you see a difference between the stanzas?
Is there an important feeling to explore in a whole stanza?	Could each stanza be about a different bit of the subject?
Is there a particular image you want to use in a stanza?	Could each stanza give a different feeling on the subject?

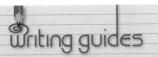

Performing a poem

- Use this planner to prepare a performance of a poem.

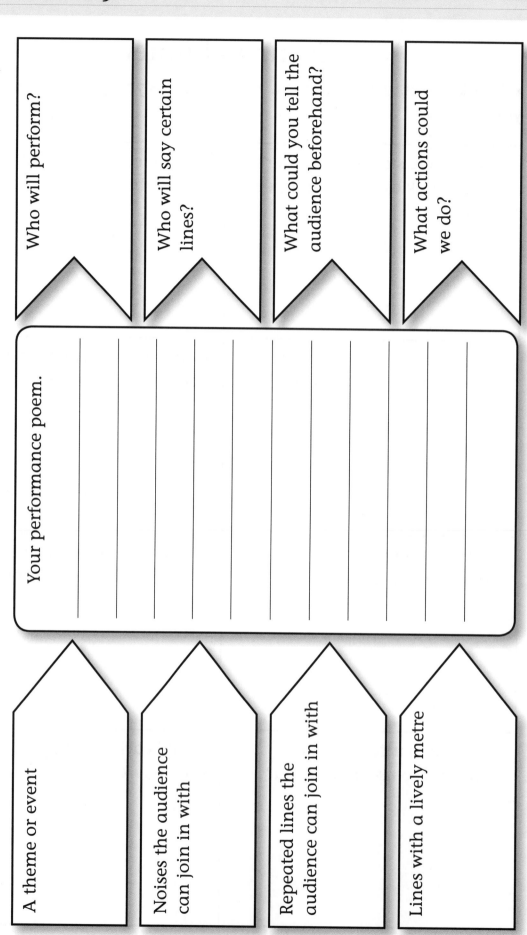

Who will perform?

Who will say certain lines?

What could you tell the audience beforehand?

What actions could we do?

Your performance poem.

A theme or event

Noises the audience can join in with

Repeated lines the audience can join in with

Lines with a lively metre

How do you say it?

● Find four points in your poem that are meant to be said in a particular way. Write down each of the four parts in the speech bubbles and then next to them explain how to say them.

How you say it...

How you say it...

How you say it...

How you say it...

Review

Revisiting a piece of work is a vital part of writing poetry, with writers often putting a vast amount of effort into a single line. The activities in this section involve peer review and teacher assessment but the focus needs to be on children's self assessment.

Self review

In this activity, the children select one line from a poem they have written. You might want to give some direction to their choice, ensuring they pick an interesting line with some potential for further work. Having selected their line, the children should write it in the space provided on photocopiable page 45 'Self review'. The task here is to make this one line a well-crafted piece of writing.

Peer review

Photocopiable page 46 'Peer review' encourages the use of review partners to help the children review and edit their written work. Organise the children to work with a partner of similar ability. Tell them to read and then review their partner's poem by answering the questions on the photocopiable sheet. Provide opportunities for feedback. Ask the children to tell their partner what they liked about their poem and to give suggestions on how it can be improved. Remind them that their comments should be constructive and supportive.

Teacher review

The grid on photocopiable page 47 'Teacher review' has been designed to enable you to assess children's progress and attainment at the end of a unit of work on poetry. It is linked to the National Curriculum's eight Assessment Focuses for writing. When reviewing children's work in relation to each Assessment Focus, it is important to include observation of speaking and listening skills as well as assessment of written work. Carrying out a review will enable you to evaluate the progress that children have made towards achieving specific learning goals. The findings of the review should be used to set individual and group learning targets and to ensure that the next steps in learning for all children are planned at the appropriate level. The review may also highlight gaps, which can be addressed by revisiting relevant lessons in earlier sections.

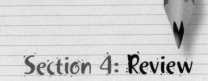
Self review

● Choose a line from a poem you have written and write it in the box.

● Now try changing some words.

Can you create a new image?

_____

_____

_____

_____

Can you change the metre?

_____

_____

_____

Can you make the line sound different? (For example, use alliteration.)

_____

_____

_____

_____

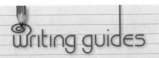

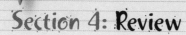

Peer review

● Read a poem written by your partner. Review the poem by answering the following questions.

Poem title: _____

Written by: _____

What is the poem about?

List some well-chosen words.

What is your favourite line?

What impact does this poem have on the reader?

Is anything unclear? Provide details.

How could this poem be improved?

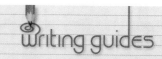
writing guides

Teacher review

	AF5 Vary sentences for clarity, purpose and effect.	AF6 Write with technical accuracy of syntax and punctuation in phrases, clauses and sentences.	AF3 Organise and present whole texts effectively, sequencing and structuring information, ideas and events.	AF1 Write imaginative, interesting and thoughtful texts.	AF7 Select appropriate and effective vocabulary.
LEVEL 3	Reliance mainly on simply structured sentences, variation with support, *for example, some complex sentences.* Some limited variation in use of tense and verb forms, not always secure.	Some accurate use of demarcation, within poetic line structure, with full stops, capital letters, question and exclamation marks.	Some attempt to sequence ideas or material logically, clustering similar ideas into sections of the poem.	Some appropriate ideas and content included. Some attempt to elaborate on basic information or events, *for example, nouns expanded by simple adjectives.*	Some words selected for effect or occasion.
LEVEL 4	Variation in sentence construction, with accurate use of different tense and verb forms to suit the poem.	Sentences demarcated accurately throughout the text, while maintaining line variety appropriate to poetic form. Commas used in descriptive lists and occasionally to mark clauses, although not always accurately.	Ideas organised by clustering related points or by time sequence. Ideas are organised simply with a fitting opening and closing, sometimes linked. Ideas or material generally in a logical sequence, supported by stanza or other form.	Relevant ideas and content chosen. Some ideas and material developed in detail, *for example, descriptions elaborated by adverbial and expanded noun phrases.*	Some evidence of deliberate and expanded vocabulary choices to match topic.

Also available in this series:

ISBN 978-1407-11253-4

ISBN 978-1407-11265-7

ISBN 978-1407-11267-1

ISBN 978-1407-11256-5

ISBN 978-1407-11270-1

ISBN 978-1407-11248-0

ISBN 978-1407-11254-1

ISBN 978-1407-11266-4

ISBN 978-1407-11258-9

ISBN 978-1407-11268-8

ISBN 978-1407-11251-0

ISBN 978-1407-11257-2

ISBN 978-1407-11255-8

ISBN 978-1407-11269-5

ISBN 978-1407-11250-3

ISBN 978-1407-11247-3

ISBN 978-1407-11252-7

ISBN 978-1407-11264-0

ISBN 978-1407-11249-7

ISBN 978-1407-11260-2

ISBN 978-1407-11261-9

ISBN 978-1407-11263-3

ISBN 978-1407-11259-6

ISBN 978-1407-11262-6

To find out more, call: **0845 603 9091** or visit our website: **www.scholastic.co.uk**